VENUS' DAUGHTER

VENUS' DAUGHTER

Meghan Swaby

SCIROCCO DRAMA

Venus' Daughter
first published 2022 by Scirocco Drama
An imprint of J. Gordon Shillingford Publishing Inc.
© 2022 Meghan Swaby

Scirocco Drama Editor: Glenda MacFarlane
Cover design by Doowah Design
Author photo by Chris Frampton
Production photos by Lyon Smith

Printed and bound in Canada on 100% post-consumer recycled paper.
We acknowledge the financial support of the Manitoba Arts Council and
The Canada Council for the Arts for our publishing program.

Production inquiries to:
The Edward G Agency
Sandie Newton
19 Isabella Street, Toronto, ON, M4Y 1M7
416-960-8683 x 223
president@edwardagency.com

Library and Archives Canada Cataloguing in Publication

Title: Venus' daughter / Meghan Swaby.
Names: Swaby, Meghan, author.
Description: A play.
Identifiers: Canadiana (print) 20220196842 | Canadiana (ebook) 20220196869 |
ISBN 9781927922965
  (softcover) | ISBN 9781990737138 (HTML)
Classification: LCC PS8637.W32 V46 2022 | DDC C812/.6—dc23

J. Gordon Shillingford Publishing
P.O. Box 86, RPO Corydon Avenue, Winnipeg, MB Canada R3M 3S3

For Sara Baartman, Mummy, Tasha and Malia.

Meghan Swaby

Meghan Swaby is a first-generation Jamaican Canadian actor and playwright based in Toronto. Her play *Venus' Daughter* was produced by Obsidian Theatre in 2016 and was included on The SureFire List (Playwrights Guild of Canada) as one of the top 23 recommended plays in Canada. She has participated in playwriting residencies at various theatres and festivals, including Nightwood Theatre, Obsidian Theatre, Diaspora Dialogues, Playwrights' Workshop Montreal, the Stratford Festival, Noteworthy, and First Drafts. Her work has been performed internationally and was included as part of *50in50: Writing Black Women Into Existence* at the Billie Holiday Theatre (Brooklyn, NY). She has been awarded grants from the Canada Council for the Arts, the Ontario Arts Council and the Toronto Arts Council for her writing.

Meghan is a graduate of the University of Windsor (BFA–Acting), and an alumna of the International Actors Fellowship at Shakespeare's Globe (UK).

She is the co-creator of *Beneath the Ceiba Tree*, a podcast about Caribbean folklore.

Acknowledgements

Thank you to Mel Hague, Obsidian Theatre, Tania Senewiratne, Michael Sinclair, Luke Reese, Leah Simone Bowen, ahdri zhina mandiela and the rAi'zn ensemble (b current), d'bi young, Yemoya International Artist residency, Nightwood Theatre, Anna Chatterton, Audrey Dwyer, Natasha Greenblatt, Jordi Mand, Aisha Sasha John, Natasha Aidyana Morris and the Piece of Mine Festival, Rebecca Fissaha, and Diaspora Dialogues.

To the many incredible artists who've participated in the countless workshops over the years, thank you for sharing your hearts/minds: Dian Marie Bridge, Marika Warner, Sophia Walker, Sabryn Rock, Marcel Stewart, Mumbi Tindyebwa Otu, Virgilia Griffith, Peter N Bailey, Sebastien Heins, Tsholo Khalema, Esie Mensah, Tawiah McCarthy, Kaleb Alexander, and Akosua Amo Adem.

Thank you to the Toronto Arts Council, the Ontario Arts Council and the Canada Council for the Arts.

My utmost gratitude to Philip Akin who invested in and nurtured my voice as a playwright; who committed to me when I jumped into this world and has made me a better artist.

Foreword

It is impossible for me to speak about *Venus' Daughter* on my own. Although I lived with this work for many years as a dramaturge, when I was asked to write this introduction it felt vital to reflect on the play along with members of the community who brought it to life. Consequently, this foreword incorporates conversations with Meghan Swaby, the playwright, and with Akosua Amo-Adem, the actor who not only originated the role of Venus in its premiere but also worked with us during the play's development process. I thank them for their generosity with their time, and for their thoughts.

What is *Venus' Daughter* about, you might ask? I will offer you a few premises:

- *Denise, a young Black Jamaican-Canadian woman, reveals her obsession with comparing and scrutinizing bodies while exposing a lack of connection with her own.*

- *Venus, the ancestral embodiment of Sara Baartman (The Hottentot Venus, Sara "Saartjie" Baartman), appears to Denise, a young Black woman, and shares the joys and sorrows of her storied life.*

- *Denise must return to her mother's first home in Jamaica to bury her grandmother. Over the course of the Nine Nights following her grandmother's passing, Denise is sent on a journey of self-discovery by her ancestors to find a home within herself.*

Venus' Daughter is all of these things, none of them, and in the end is much greater than the sum of its parts.

I believe that in the process of writing *Venus' Daughter*, Swaby tapped into the profound core of Black womanhood as a continuous journey through many ages, generations, and realms of consciousness, a journey animated by poetry, spirituality, and the connectivity of peoples through a complex diasporic web. I cannot overemphasize the fearlessness that embarking on that journey takes; to continue to peel back layers upon layers of the lived realities of feelings, sensations, histories, and characters to their raw essential parts, to bring that to a reality on the page, and to lift that journey onto the stage. The depth of Swaby's work on this play is extraordinary and fills me with pride.

I want to provide you with a series of frames or lenses with which to read *Venus' Daughter*. Each could be described as a "theme" within the work, but I prefer to think of them as entryways into the world that Swaby has offered us. This is not a complete list. None is truer than the other. In combination they create the magic of *Venus' Daughter*. They are:

- *Humour and Grief*
- *History*
- *Culture*
- *Bodies*

On Humour and Grief

It would be a mistake to view this work as not filled to the brim with humour and joy. When you read it, I challenge you to seek the humour and the joy—it is through those shades and hues that the darkness and grief become truly visible. Meghan says:

> I think the humour is essential to this work. We need those respites, in art and in life. When you are burnt out, when there's a well of emotion—if you don't have those ways of releasing it, you try to just keep it down. But it needs to pass through, however you do that: sweat it out, laugh it out, cry it out. I do feel like in this work, humour serves that purpose.

Grief is a core driver of the play. As you read, I invite you to consider: How do we encounter loss in our lives? Both the loss felt in times of death and transition in our lives, and the grief for losses that we can't quite articulate—loss of purpose, place, or community?

On History

Meghan says:

> *It started with an image. It may have even been a YouTube video. It was like, "Do you know the story of Sara Baartman?" I remember specifically those political satirical cartoons from England in the early 1800s — I was feeling curious and disgusted and angry and all those things. I felt a heat in my chest. And then I was inhaling anything that mentioned the name Hottentot Venus or Sara Baartman. I began writing and filling notebooks with research. Then I needed to translate the research into the world-building of the play and bring it back to the self and my personal connection to the image.*

Venus' Daughter came from a place of deep and faithful research into the life and story of Sara Baartman. It is the genesis and nexus of this work and is deeply indebted to her journey. As the play grew, it became clear that it was not so much a sharing a of piece of tragic and painful history as it was a receptacle for the immense living echoes of Baartman's spiritual impact across time and space.

On Bodies

Akosua says:

> *You know, I'm from Ghana; my people are Ashanti people.*
>
> *And so there's a very specific way that the female body is viewed in Ghana and a lot of African cultures, they appreciate the booty, the thickness of a woman.*
>
> *And for me, it was interesting, having to play a character who was revered for and known for her derrière.*
>
> *It was the first time that I had engaged with a play that actually talked about my body type, or the body types of women who looked like me, and who came from the same place that I came from. And the first time that I could have those kinds of dialogues and that conversation about the Black female body with reference to a piece of art I was working on.*

This piece, for all the poetry, magic, and time in liminal spaces, is rooted in the experience of the Black female body. It is not only an ethereal journey, but a deep physical and sensorial experience.

On Culture

Akosua says:

> It is written from a Jamaican-Canadian perspective. Jamaican first, Canadian second. So it requires having a grasp of the cultural space, and how the culture influences the text; how these layers of culture influence the journey of Denise and the structure of the work.

This piece, like many new Canadian works, is the culmination of vast diasporic journeys influenced and impacted by colonization. The relationship between Denise, Sara Baartman, Jamaica, Canada, and South Africa is many hundreds of years in the making—this piece and its characters sit in the eye of these cultural storms. And, I believe, it invites a curiosity from its audiences into how these constellations of histories and peoples find connection and belonging.

When I reflect upon the process of working with Meghan Swaby on *Venus' Daughter,* I am struck by the amount of joy that this piece brought to me as it grew. I am also reminded of my own growth, Meghan's growth, and the growth of the generous artists who brought this work to life.

It is a pleasure and a privilege to introduce you to this incredible play, which I hope brings you the same joy, provocation, and lasting curiosity that it has brought to me and the many artists who worked on it.

Mel Hague
January 2022

Mel Hague is a Toronto-based curator and dramaturge and is currently the Associate Artistic Director at Canadian Stage Company.

Akosua Amo-Adem is an actor, writer, and director based in Toronto.

Production History

Venus' Daughter was initially developed through Nightwood Theatre's Write from the Hip Program in 2010. From there, it became part of Obsidian Theatre's development series, and was produced by Obsidian Theatre at the Theatre Centre in Toronto, Ontario, in February 2016.

Cast

TORTOISE .... Akosua Amo-Adem
SARA
VENUS
CUSTOMER #1
MUMMY
FLIGHT ATTENDANT

DENISE .... Meghan Swaby
DOCTOR #1

CESAR .... Kaleb Alexander
YOUNG CUSTOMER
DR. DUNLOP
THE KID
NINE-YEAR-OLD DENISE
GEORGE CUVIER

Creative Team

PHILIP AKIN – Director

MICHAEL SINCLAIR – Stage Manager

PATRICK LAVENDER – Production Manager

JOE PAGNAN – Set and Costume Design

KAITLIN HICKEY – Lighting and Projection Design

LYON SMITH – Sound Design

ESIE MENSAH – Movement Design

TAWIAH M'CARTHY – Assistant Director

SARA ALLISON – Apprentice Stage Manager

Venus (Akosua Amo-Adem) has a last moment with
Denise (Meghan Swaby). Photo by Lyon Smith.

Sara Baartman (Akosua Amo-Adem) is displayed
on an examination table before Dr. Alexander Dunlop
(Kaleb Alexander) and Doctor #1/Denise (Meghan Swaby).
Photo by Lyon Smith.

Denise (Meghan Swaby) is unknowingly coaxed
into a dance with Venus (Akosua Amo-Adem).
Photo by Lyon Smith.

Characters

TORTOISE:
A dark-skinned Black woman, ageless. The guide.

SARA BAARTMAN:
A dark-skinned Black woman, 30s, her hips are wide like the base of a mountain, her thighs thick and strong like the trunk of a tree. The catalyst.

VENUS:
A dark-skinned Black woman, early 30s, an Ancestor. The provocateur.

DENISE:
A Black woman, 30 years old, apologetic, her body is similar to SARA BAARTMAN's. She distracts herself with pain to avoid change.

CUSTOMER:
Late 60s, a customer in Denise's workplace.

FLIGHT ATTENDANT:
Late 20s, Venus in disguise.

MUMMY:
Early 70s, Jamaican, Denise's mother.
Small, mighty, and unapologetic.

CESAR:
A light-skinned Black man, early 40s. His family owned Sara Baartman; he's part of the "Free Blacks" community in Cape Town. The master of ceremony.

DR. DUNLOP:
A Scotsman, 54, a former surgeon who takes Sara Baartman to London along with Cesar.
An opportunist.

YOUNG CUSTOMER:
A white woman, late 20s, wishes she had a closer proximity to Blackness.

THE KID:
A yute, almost 10 years old, a natural hustler.

UNCLE PASON:
Black, Jamaican, 62, Denise's uncle
and Mummy's brother.

NINE-YEAR-OLD DENISE:
Denise's inner child. Hopeful.

DR. GEORGE CUVIER:
A French scientist, white, 47. Founder of
comparative anatomy; the man who performs the
posthumous dissection of Sara Baartman's body.

DOCTOR #1:
A senior doctor observing Dr. Dunlop's surgical theatre.

All characters are Black and are to be played by Black actors.

For the actors playing Venus and Denise, it is integral to the
storytelling that their bodies mirror one other.

Sara/Venus/Tortoise is played by the same actor.
When she is SARA (Sara Baartman) she is reliving
moments from her past. When she speaks as VENUS
(Hottentot Venus) it is from having lived through
tragic events, but she never feels sorry for herself.
She is direct, purposeful, heightened, and melodic,
as if her words are plucked from another world.
TORTOISE is the mythological combination
of both women, never confined to space/time.

Suggestions for Doubling

Denise/Doctor #1

Venus/Tortoise/Sara Baartman/Customer/Mummy/
Flight Attendant/ Nine-Year-Old Denise*

Cesar/Young Customer/The Kid/ Dr. Dunlop/
Dr. George Cuvier/Nine-Year-Old Denise*

---

* Nine-Year-Old Denise can be played by either the actor who plays
Venus or the actor who plays Cesar.

Notes on style

Text between dialogue in ALL CAPS is choreography.
It can be spoken or silent.

Italicized text within a character's speech is a
kind of possession, a linguistic déjà vu.

Bold & italicized text within a character's speech
indicates that it is heavily rhythmic.

Production Notes

There are no blackouts between scenes.
This is a play in two parts. Each part flows into the next.
The progression of scenes mirrors that of the
Jamaican tradition of Nine Night.

Nine Night: A Jamaican wake where family and
friends of the deceased gather for nine nights
for a celebration of life. There is sharing of
food and drink to ensure the duppy (spirit)
gets a proper send-off.

Mami Wata (mother water): (ma = truth/ wisdom)
Water spirit and healer of physical and spiritual ills.
She is the embodiment of dangers, desires, and fertility.
People are attracted to and fearful of her destructive power.
Beautiful, protective, and seductive. When one receives
a calling from mami wata, depression, spiritual
psychosis, and dreams are intensified.

PART ONE
One Night: Nine Night

A bare stage. Twilight. A place where the dead communicate with the living. The sound of fierce waves smashing up against the earth crescendos and stops. A white TORTOISE crosses the stage.

TORTOISE:

When we are the closest to the end our bodies know exactly what to do to carry us over.

Our bodies refuse food because on the other side a feast awaits us. We talk to people from the past, present, future—unseen to your eye. We stop moving the way you want us to, show up without your permission, and remain silent when expected to speak. We need to save up our energy for the flight. We flick, pluck, and pick beneath sheets. Leaving behind fragments of our old lives. We no longer have pockets to keep them in. We are getting ready to leave our old lives and let our bodies sink, buried beneath.

Earth. Water. Stone.

Once your body is under the feet of your loved ones, your soul goes up like so... body stays down like so...and the spirit (di duppy) roams 'round dem yard for nine nights. On the last night, there is a celebration where family and friends gather from all over to laugh, talk, cry, sing, dance, clap, eat an' drink under the stars. When the sun comes up, people go back to dem yard and de duppy can go off to its new home, its last home.

We finally go home to ourselves. Eager, excited like children, curious, hungry, bawling, stretching, hoping, hopping... *up!* On tippy-scrunched toesies tight—*UP!* Fingers sprawled, head-neck cranked, veins bulging *up ma, mama, mami UP!*

A familiar stranger pulls you like a powerful undercurrent swooping you away without warning.

I reach out to scoop, pull, wrap, hold, grab all my babies that did not pass through my legs but share my blood, flesh and scars.

Flight!

> *Four sides of a cage slowly erupt from the ground trapping the white TORTOISE. She is now hidden by a delicious velvet drapery that hangs in front.*

Two Night: The Show

> *1810. London, England. Piccadilly Circus. Inside an overcrowded, wet, loud, smoky cabaret. CESAR stands onstage with a whip in his hand. He is the Master of Ceremonies.*

CESAR: Good evening! You have made a good choice, my friends. You are all very good people, I can see that. You have had enough of the mindless, low-brow entertainment that floods the streets of this great city. You want more. My friends, I am happy to share with you...my secret. Once you lay eyes upon this wondrous creature, you will become entranced, cast under her spell. Tonight, you will experience sights usually reserved for explorers, scientists and doctors. You, my friends, are among the first to witness a specimen so close to nature that the red dirt of Africa still rests under her toes. Fresh, from Africa...

A woman of extraordinary shape and make.

Rescued, from the dark, mysterious "barbaric wilderness of Africa."

I present to you...

THE...HOTTENTOT...VENUS!

> *CESAR rips off drapery to reveal a woman in a metal cage. Her face is pressed up against the bars as she shakes the cage. The woman is SARA BAARTMAAN, the woman in the posters, aka "The Hottentot Venus." Her hips are wide like the base of a mountain and her thighs are thick and strong like the trunk of a tree.*
>
> *SARA pounds one foot into the ground, the other foot, and then both feet at the same time. This causes the floor to crack and then separate. Everyone gets swallowed up, except SARA. She continues to dance, arms reaching up to the stars, legs clapping open and shut like wings about to take flight. A thumping bass vibrates from the floor. She goes back inside the cage. It transforms into a dressing room.*

Three Night: Denise at Work

Present day. Downtown Toronto. In the hallway of the dressing rooms at The Bay. DENISE, an employee, is hunched over, looking through the crack of the dressing room door at the customer.

DENISE: 38-34-52

Waist-to-hip ratio. Rump to crown. Thighs.

Some look like flipped-up mountains, peaks pointed down, expanded widewide

whitewine make mountain wide thighs quiver shake seize grip tight.

Ripples in your hips make my mouth whip words foreign to my tongue

(To herself.) Stop it.

I can measure with my mind's eye a number tight to truth.

Eighteen stretch marks across the abdomen. Thick, like mine. I can run my fingers along the ridges. Each ridge bumpier than the last. Like you were clawed by a beast and these are your battle wounds. Cocoa butter doesn't stand a chance against those wounds. Wounds from past lives. They show up on the present body and live in the now. Pay close attention and you can see the story in them. This one is a sad story. The lines wrap round your whole waist and stop under the bust. Someone wanted parts of you without your permission and branded your body to remind you so. Like hot metal screaming for skin their desire seared your skin, cooked you, you cried mouth open to the sky, thinking there was no pain more bearable than what you were going through. But this reminder comes a close second. The pain stopped. This kept on your body. Cannot be removed, even worse, you have to learn to love it. Love the thing that a monster gifted to you. Is this your story?

We are master trick-sisters
of changing our bodies
to make them nicer to our eyes.

So many types of bodies I forget exist. We cover them so well. We filter away flaws and find figure-flattering frocks to feel good.

We prize thighs that don't touch

Or demand a perfect distribution of just enough fat to be baby phat fly.

And if you are not one of the two, you disappear.

Parts of me have actually disappeared beneath fabric.

I glare in front of mirrors and beg back a lost fragment.

To rediscover parts of you when sneaking peeks at others in dressing rooms.

CUSTOMER: Deeeeaaar....

DENISE: Are you all right in there?

CUSTOMER: Noo....oh...lawd...can you—

DENISE: Ma'am, do you need me to get you another size?

CUSTOMER: Yes... no, wait.

              This is my size. This is what I wear ... a G
              43. Me did just get fit last year.

DENISE: Ma'am, you put it on backwards

CUSTOMER: No, I didn't. I know how to wear a bra. I
              have been wearing bras since before you
              were born.

DENISE: Yes, ma'am. This here clicks in the front and
              criss-cross lies across your back.

CUSTOMER: Dat why mi nipple a show through?

DENISE: Yes.

CUSTOMER: These blasted things shouldn't be so hard
              to wear, man!" (Cut "Well,")

DENISE: I agree.

CUSTOMER: Well, you show me how dis ting haffe
              work.

              *DENISE unbuttons the front clasps of
              the bra. She notices a tortoise necklace the
              woman is wearing, which is caught on the
              bra strap.*

CUSTOMER: It's the oldest thing I own.

              Me swear every year dem a jus grow and
              grow.

DENISE: Well...weight gain can affect bra sizing—

CUSTOMER: (*Defensive.*) Me nah gain any weight. Just
              me breasts.

When I was your age I loved it. All the attention...me swear it did mek me waist look nice and tight. Me would wear low low neck, lace, all dem sintings!

DENISE: You can still wear those things, you know.

CUSTOMER: Cyan't even lie good. Who gwan look pon me wid these droopy tings, dem long like a'what.

DENISE: Not at all. You still got it.

CUSTOMER: Oh mi know dat, me darling. Me mudda did bless me with nice skin, at least me have dat. "Black don't crack." But all de good tings dat go so, now drag pon de floor! Just you wait. See, you young and fulla life. Don't waste time cry'n in de mirror bout dis lump here dat crease d'ere. It's good, enjoy your body now, before it starts moving faster than you ready.

DENISE: Yes, ma'am.

Here, put your arms straight out.

There.

CUSTOMER: You must tink I mad.

DENISE: You're...vivacious.

CUSTOMER: *(Kiss teeth.)* "Vivacious."

Okay...

Dem supposed to look so high?

DENISE: "Lift and separate."

CUSTOMER: You have it inna black?

DENISE: Yup. How's the fit?

CUSTOMER: It aright...

DENISE: The straps? Not too tight?

CUSTOMER: Mek it a liccle more loose.

DENISE: Better?

CUSTOMER: Mmhum...

DENISE: I'm gonna go get you the one in black.

                 DENISE turns to leave.

CUSTOMER: *(Shouting after her.)* And if you have a
                 bottom to match it, bring it out!

                 *DENISE exits and re-enters periodically
                 with more and more black bras and
                 underwear sets. Her cell phone goes off;
                 she looks at it, then ignores it.*

Three Night/Part B: Going Home

DENISE: *(V.O.)* He, you've reached Dee's cell, leave
                 your message at—

                 Beep.

MUMMY: Denise? You mus be at work, you should
                 carry you phone on you for emergency me
                 tell you dat all'di time, *(Sucks teeth.)* Me
                 have some bad news ya'... Mayve—

                 Beep.

DENISE: *(V.O.)* Hey, you've reached Dee's cell, leave
                 your message at—

                 Beep.

MUMMY:	Di stupid ting a cut me off man, me cyant even leave message, yuh need fa call Rogers an getti fix. Denise? Mayve dead. She dead off, man. She mussa just doze right off inna ar' bed. We haffe go down... She just ...gone. Me feel fi cry. Lawd e? Call me when you on break nah. Oh, it's Mummy.

Three Night/Part C: Denise Still at Work

	Present (same day). Toronto. Back at work. DENISE is hunched, looking through the gap in the dressing room door at a pretty YOUNG CUSTOMER, played convincingly by the actor who plays CESAR.
DENISE:	30-22-33. Pants looped down round your ankles. Bright red tags show off your brand and size. "Lucky 00." You're a lucky double-negative using pads to stretch out your shape.
YOUNG CUSTOMER:	Do you have anything with more of a push-up?
DENISE:	You would have to go to Victoria's Secret for that. This is all we have.
YOUNG CUSTOMER:	I hate my flat chest, I just wish I could move the fat from my ass to my boobs. You know? My boyfriend calls me Saskatchewan... such a douchebag ... I'm flat like the prairies. I know, we got in this huge thing over it—you have a boyfriend? *(Doesn't wait for response.)* I won't take shit from guys. You know how it is, girl, "I'm a 10," I said that, I am a fucking 10, you know? Fucking men, no, boys, they're all boys.

Butlookit, since I got this tho *(Snaps her booty pop pants)*. it's like he can't keep his hands off me, calls me his mini "kim-bea-lo." you know... like Kim, Beyonce & J-Lo, 'cause look...

The YOUNG CUSTOMER starts twerking.

DENISE: That's ...fast.

YOUNG CUSTOMER: I know, right. Now I have such a "ghetto booty" ...Well, you know, for a white girl.

YOUNG CUSTOMER returns to the dressing room and tosses a dozen bras out from the change room. This continues. Hundreds of bras, thongs, girdles, Spanx, nylons, and silicon cutlets are whipped over her door, hitting DENISE.

DENISE: Do you need another size?

YOUNG CUSTOMER: Nothing is fitting the way I want it to. I shouldn't have had breakfast. I'm so bloated. I'm on this gluten-free/thing and I'm finding it really—

DENISE: Sure, okay, I love gluten. Do you need another size?!

DENISE snaps out of that moment to speak directly to the audience. As she goes through the list of names, the YOUNG CUSTOMER strikes a series of selfies showcasing her best "ASSets."

The first line of A Tribe Called Quest's "Da Booty" is either spoken or seen in a projection above the action.

Music cue: "Question: What is it that everyone has, that some pirates and thieves try to take?"

DENISE: I'm sorry, but did you know, when you look up "ass" in urban dictionary you get like 51 different names? I Googled it; apple bottom, backside, bubble butt, ba-donka-donk, caboose, clapper, cushion, derrière, donk, fanny, gluteus maximus, heinie, horse's petute, hump, junk in the trunk, matako, moneymaker, onion, patootie, pooper, pooter, rump, tail feather, tooshy, trunk, tokus, tush, whoopie cakes—

A rhythm of muffled drums begins to rise from the ground, we have heard these sounds before. DENISE is distracted, losing her place in the list.

—dookie maker, duff, fanny, horse's petute, keester, posterior, arse...

*A giant silhouette of VENUS appears in the background, between DENISE and the YOUNG CUSTOMER. Summoned from this incantation. VENUS is larger than life. YOUNG CUSTOMER melts into the darkness. Words in **bold quotations** become a rap verse (Dirty South) performed by CESAR.*

broad in the beam / **"damn baby, bounce dat—"**

bum / **"yum pu-tang, sweet juicy dang"**

buns / **"hot out the oven, let me get close, show daddy dat crack cake"**

ghetto booty / **"mammy sugar sex me sweetie"**

caboose / *"sweet tooth, keep it tight no use if you loose"*

The ground beneath DENISE's feet rumbles. DENISE is terrified but fights to conceal it. VENUS emerges from the shadows, still.

VENUS recites:

VENUS:

batty behind
big booty judy bust
batty behind bruk
bounce back bonafide bubble butt
bounce back
bounce back
bounce back

VENUS dances. DENISE rushes to the mirror, like she is trying to hide from us. She is nose-to-nose with her reflection. "//bounce back" spoken by VENUS.

DENISE:

Something buzzes bounces up through my bones.
Face to mirror
// bounce back
Nose to nose
// bounce back
Heart racing
// bounce back
My heels planted, refusing to turn me around to see whatever thing that awaits.
Being watched by someone you want to see you, but are too scared to see their thoughts about you, through their eyes.

It's safer here.

It's quieter here.

DENISE starts to examine her body in the mirror, slowly removing layers of clothing till there's nothing left.

When mirrors kiss

I wedge myself between them

Beneath a green tint I can see myself stretched out, I go on for miles.

When mirrors kiss

I wedge myself between them

Stretched out making different shapes

Never one size long enough for you to catch me keep me touch me I go on for miles.

Many of the "me"s populate the room and my bigness somehow feels ...

Despite your eyes (measuring the circumference of my thighs)

I feel small and massive at the same time.

Not taking up any space because of constantly feeling out of place.

We all have these thoughts? Mine are loud and are getting crueller with age. Conversations in here aren't nice ones.

The layers of clothes/armour make their way back onto DENISE's body.

I can feel myself disappearing more and more with each passing year. Sometimes I grow and shrink depending on the room I'm in. Depending on whose legs I'm pressed up beside on a packed streetcar.

Depending on what parts get showered with praise or shame. The sharpest words can splinter through the toughest of skin. The loudest sharpest words are the ones only I can hear.

Do you remember how when you were little, you never thought anything was wrong with you until someone pointed it out? A Grade Eight field trip to Ottawa. Bored twelve-year-old boys, high on sugar, crammed on a coach bus, sticky hands passing around magazines and papers rating girls in the class over top models' faces. 1–10. Yellow highlighter keeping score: Hair, smarts, smile, lips, legs and…

> *DENISE plays the following clapping game playfully and innocently as if we are playing against her. When she gets to "K-I-S-S," she spreads her legs, so that by the third time through she struggles to stay on her feet. She repeats the game until it breaks her.*

DENISE:

"Mailman mailman, do your duty

Here comes a lady with an African booty

She can do the pom-pom, she can do the twist

but most of all she can K-I-S-S."

Four Night: Dreaming While Flying Is Dangerous

> *DENISE is on board an Air Canada flight to Jamaica, gazing out the window. A loud rumble. A typical flight attendant voice is heard from the speakers. (FLIGHT ATTENDANT is voiced by VENUS.)*

FLIGHT ATTENDANT: *(V.O.)* Good morning, passengers. It looks like we are experiencing some turbulence. Please remain seated and fasten your seat belts.

> *DENISE closes her eyes and takes a slow, deep breath.*

DENISE: *(Inhales.)* 10…Stay down stop breathe… *(Inhales.)* 10…9…8, good, 7

> *Another rumble as big as the last, lights off.*

7- 7 -sev-ssss…swear the buzzing under my feet…like a rushing river. The deceptive roughness of the clouds.

> *A loud crunch. DENISE shuts her eyes and clamps herself to her seat.*

Don't drop me in the ocean, Granny.

I'm sorry, I don't know why I said that. Never called you that till now, but I will if it helps. Forgive me for not remembering your face, but I can see parts of you in my mind, does that count? The bits of things Mummy told me about you weren't good. Never calling you "mum," just said you were "mis'narable." Two leathery thin-skinned calloused hands that ripped into the sliced-open hung goat that would soon be soup. Three large plaits, side-side and one down the back, long and silver, loose curls framing your shrinking face.

Lights come back on — it's working.

One gaping hole in your mouth where a tooth should be, but instead gammey, gummy, nothing. I still have that, at least. You do look like a mini version of Ma.

She doesn't think so... I thought you were a badgyal 'cause you went to church on the back of a kid's motorbike in your pastel blue church dress and giant black hat.

This time when I'm looking on everyone I'll take more time. It might be the last time I see them before the next funeral. I forgot to hug Aunty Shelly goodbye last time. Won't make that mistake again. Can't now. Last time I saw her, I yelled back to her and blew a kiss instead of a hug.

She gave good hugs. Perm, hair gel and vanilla...never hugged you, so I don't know what you smell like. Perm, hair gel and vanilla... I remember walking up to her house after she passed and not being able to find it 'cause there were so many cars and speakers and people selling hats and CDs and girls dancing wid unscrewed Kola Champagne in their hands. Drip drip drip pon dem bare legs and mans right unda deh fi lick e back up.

So much excitement, I forgot why I was there... I think that was the point.

FLIGHT ATTENDANT: *(V.O.)* Attention, passengers, we apologize for the inconvenience as we are experiencing some delays—

DENISE: The clouds have stopped moving. Frozen
                           in the sky, or are we falling so fast that they
                           look still? Dropping so lick quick speedy
                           clicking out the sky. So fast we freeze the
                           clouds to look still.

FLIGHT ATTENDANT: *(V.O.)* Please remain seated as we—

                           Violent turbulence throws DENISE out of
                           her chair. Stillness above the clouds. The
                           oxygen masks dislodge and dangle from
                           the ceiling.

FLIGHT ATTENDANT: *(V.O.)* We've stopped.

                           DENISE tries to shake this experience
                           from her head. She shuts her eyes, starts
                           counting and taking deep breaths.

FLIGHT ATTENDANT: *(V.O.)* Open your eyes. You can't block this
                           out.

DENISE: No... I'm doing it again. This is not—

FLIGHT ATTENDANT: *(V.O.)* There is nothing wrong with you.
                           Open your eyes.

                           A moment.

DENISE: Where did everyone else go?

FLIGHT ATTENDANT: *(V.O.)* They are still sleeping. You are the
                           only one awake, so lift your head and look
                           up.

DENISE: Who / are you?

FLIGHT ATTENDANT: *(V.O.)* /You know me

DENISE: Who are you?

FLIGHT ATTENDANT: *(V.O.)* You know me.

DENISE: Can I see you?

FLIGHT ATTENDANT: *(V.O.)* Not yet. Soon enough.

DENISE: What happens now?

> *NINE-YEAR-OLD DENISE (Can be played by the actor who plays CESAR.) runs and almost bumps into DENISE. Her hair is a mess. DENISE recognizes herself right away.*

DENISE: No way—

You look different than how I remember myself looking. Oh god, and that sweater... Come here, let me fix your hair.

> *NINE-YEAR-OLD DENISE hangs her head, walks over to DENISE and sits between her legs. DENISE begins to fix her hair.*

DENISE: How old are you—or am I—right now?

NINE-YEAR-OLD: Nine and three-quarters!

DENISE: Good.

NINE-YEAR-OLD: Why?

DENISE: Trust me.

You were on that plane?

NINE-YEAR-OLD: Not really. It's hard to explain.

I came out of the turbulence.

DENISE: You came out of the turbulence. Right...I, um...I can't finish your hair—

NINE-YEAR-OLD: You didn't even do anything. Just finish—

DENISE: It's too nappy, I can't fix it!

NINE-YEAR-OLD: Geez, okay.

A moment.

DENISE: Sorry…my head is—I don't know what's wrong with me.

NINE-YEAR-OLD: You're just in the air.

DENISE: Feel like I'm slipping

NINE-YEAR-OLD: You're still moving, though.

Beat.

NINE-YEAR-OLD: Oh, I'm supposed to give this to you.

> *NINE-YEAR-OLD DENISE takes the tortoise necklace out of her pocket, the same one we saw the woman in the dressing room wearing. The string of the necklace gets caught on an orange Tamagotchi, Dr. Pepper Lip Smackers, and a Glitter Boondoggle necklace.*

DENISE: Where did you get this?

NINE-YEAR-OLD: A woman gave it to me. She traded me a Jos Louis, to make sure I put it straight into your hands. She said it was super old.

DENISE: Why is it wet? What she look like?

NINE-YEAR-OLD: I don't know—

DENISE: Did she have an accent?

NINE-YEAR-OLD: Mmm, I think so, I don't remember though. She was short, dark skin, oh and she had a really big— *(Making the shape of a big butt with her hands.)*

DENISE: Okay okay…I've seen this necklace before. It smells like wet sand—

NINE-YEAR-OLD:	If you put your ear under the tortoise shell, you can hear the waves of the ocean.

They both listen to the tortoise necklace and smile.

NINE-YEAR-OLD:	Sweet, huh?
DENISE:	Totally.

NINE-YEAR-OLD DENISE puts the necklace on DENISE. They both pause and look around. Expecting something major to happen.

NINE-YEAR-OLD:	Do you hear anything?
DENISE:	What?
NINE-YEAR-OLD:	Shhh. (*Listens.*) 'Kay, maybe if we close our eyes…

They both stand side by side holding hands with their eyes shut tight. A bright glow pulses behind them and there is the echo of a low rumble.

NINE-YEAR-OLD:	Yeeees.

NINE-YEAR-OLD DENISE goes to leave but DENISE latches on to her arm.

DENISE:	Whoa, whoa, whoa. Where you going?
NINE-YEAR-OLD:	Ow, hey! Don't worry. She'll be here soon.
DENISE:	Please, I can't … you don't know this yet but I—we—the "I" now isn't strong, or brave—
NINE-YEAR-OLD:	You're going to be fine.
DENISE:	I'm not the "thrive in the face of adversity" type. I don't do surprises—

NINE-YEAR-OLD: There is no reason to be—

DENISE: I get these …it feels like the only air my body can take in is never enough. I'm not good with not knowing. I'm not a brave person, I stopped being brave a long time ago.

NINE-YEAR-OLD: Let me go.

DENISE: Don't leave me alone.

NINE-YEAR-OLD: Okay.

You want to play a game I just learned?

DENISE: Sure.

NINE-YEAR-OLD: Okay, you don't know what I'm going to say and you have to try at talk the same time I talk. But I'm gonna talk really slow so you—

DENISE: I know this.

NINE-YEAR-OLD: 'Kay, good. I'll start. No matter what, keep going even if it's bad.

They speak together.

NINE-YEAR-OLD-
& DENISE: There was once a girl who was born to no one. She lived in a time where there was only darkness…

NINE-YEAR-OLD DENISE breaks off into the story. Perhaps DENISE is mouthing some of the words.

NINE-YEAR-OLD: She could not feel where her body ended in space because she did not have one shape. One night she awoke from her sleep because she saw a bright light. She was no longer alone.

As DENISE listens, she is transported into the story.

She tried to close her eyes to make it go away, but that didn't work. The light copied itself inside her. It was pulling her. She couldn't stop moving towards it, she looked around and saw that she now had hands. Long thick fleshy sticks that stretched out. She looked down and noticed fleshy flat broad feet dragging, skidding over stones. She was starting to fill parts of herself in. All because of this mysterious light. She could feel parts of her coming together—and she became stronger.

Even though she was scared to stare into the light that had changed her, she did, it burned her eyes to look, but she knew this light was powerful. Suddenly she could see something.

DENISE takes over telling the story in words not her own.

DENISE: A face.

VENUS emerges.

Soft, round, super-moon white eyes.

Skin, dark and shimmering. Lines that predict the folds of skin.

A long neck that cradles thick deliciously kinky hair on one side.

When you scan more of her, you see she has no legs like you and me.

Legs bound from cuts that healed over, giving birth to scar tissue.

The woman moves slow, and with ease.

Her hands are hard, long and hot,

Moving closer—I don't care to hear the sear of my newly formed skin.

Her hand outstretched,

My skin, still hot, cools to her watery touch.

Her teeth, tongue, mouth *clicks — cackles — cracks.*

The whites of her eyes leap out and steal my breath. She is light and large, always in motion. She smells like saltwater, morning lakes and raging rivers. I look down at my feet and they are down past the grass, mud, rock,

feet sinking *deeper and deeper.*

Eyes watered, skin wind whipped, chest heavy hot buzzing like fire instead ...

I *click-crackle-crack* my head back

Stand solid tall

feet dig deeper into the mud

past the roots and rocks and worms

Mouth wide to the sky—

> *A thunderous crack erupts from DENISE's mouth. VENUS and NINE-YEAR-OLD DENISE are swallowed up.*

> *Darkness.*

Music creeps in like a crack of light and swells. It is possibly a song that SARA BAARTMAAN grew up playing on a Sankey. Then, over time, the music morphs into mento (Jamaican calypso), then to dancehall. DENISE dances, thinking she is alone. Her movements start small then grow with surprising confidence. She thrusts, shakes, drops, swerving her hips to hug everything around her. As DENISE floats, VENUS emerges and coaxes her.

They dance with each other, DENISE still believing that she is alone, but VENUS guiding all of DENISE's movements. Very occasionally, they dance together. VENUS is always three beats ahead.

End of Part One

PART TWO
Five Night: Welcome to Sangster (MBJ)

> *DENISE and her MUMMY are wedged in her uncle's car while it creeps through a river of traffic. It is loud and humid. Nothing around them is moving...except a KID in tattered clothes squeezing through traffic on a motorbike. THE KID is about nine years old.*

THE KID: Beg you fa' liccle change ma' me. One western dolla! Please ma'me, anyting to help. Me nah eat ma'me, me cyan't see good, me belly a shriiiiink.

DENISE: Me? Um...

THE KID: Ya'av one western dolla cyan lend?

DENISE: I have a toonie—

THE KID: Please ma'me, me hungry hungry hungry s'tell. Me lose me vision inna dis here eye/ *(Continues to talk through DENISE's line.)*

DENISE: /Shouldn't you not be riding ...

THE KID: An me cyan't go back to school 'cause de teacha.... di man dem kill ar' off and dem shoot up di place and mek de school close off. Me never learn fi read or write. Me mummy dead, me daddy dead, dem even kill off "Scruffy," me puss. Just me liccle grannyma and she not gwan last long. *(Snaps fingers.)* What 'bout de necklace?

> *THE KID sticks his little skinny hand in the window of the car, trying to take it. DENISE slaps THE KID's hand. Harder than she should.*

DENISE: Little shit! Sorry. No, not sorry. Get your—

THE KID is really blind in one eye and has a horrible aim. He accidentally grabs DENISE's breast. Keeps his little hand there…

DENISE: GET YOUR HANDS—

Car swerves. THE KID screams.

Shit, you okay?

THE KID: Yuh try fi kill me!

DENISE: Don't stick your skinny arms into moving cars. Plus, I wouldn't have screamed if you—you grabbed my—how old are you? Like seven?

THE KID: Nine n'a half.

DENISE: Whatever—you don't grab women. What's wrong with you? No home training.

THE KID: I don't have a home.

DENISE: I DON'T CARE. You're trying to hustle me. I'm JAMAICAN! Go find some white tourists.

THE KID: Dem woulda av' nicer tings pon dem. Dis here necklace? It not even design'ah name brand, cyant even sell dat ugly sinting suh, booooy it big and ugly.

DENISE: I hope you get run off a cliff.

THE KID: Me cyan tek whateva dat sinting pon yuh wrist.

Me neva did really want to feel you up. Me like me gyal dem wid more breasts. An you have liccle bitty—

DENISE: What do you even know about… I am fine for my size. (Why am I telling you this?) THAT, what you did—is a violation of of of boundaries, of my comfort level, sooo beyond appropriate. I'm not an animal, you can't stick your little grimy hands and grope me—

THE KID: Yuh from a foreign?

DENISE: (Breathes.) Yes, first generation Canadian-Jama—

THE KID: So like, near New York?

DENISE: No, up like…. you know Drake?

THE KID: Me love—

DENISE: There. Toronto.

THE KID: Me neva even did tink Canada did have Black people.

Six Night: Granny's House

Granny's house. DENISE is sitting on the edge of a bed looking at her phone. MUMMY is behind her, unpacking clothes from her giant suitcase.

DENISE: I don't think they like me.

MUMMY: Dem nah know yuh fi not like you. You family.

DENISE: If we died, they wouldn't hop on a plane and come bury us.

MUMMY: I know.

DENISE: So why we rush over—

MUMMY: You see my—

DENISE: It's in the plastic bag, under—

MUMMY: Oh me fin' it, me have it…

DENISE: Yvonne, Kelly, Charm, Basil, Nelly, Dan—
            Dion, what's his son's name?

MUMMY: The dark one?

DENISE: Ya.

MUMMY: Junior? Dat one dead off.

DENISE: Oh, when?

MUMMY: Long time ago.

DENISE: Too hard to keep track. They all look so
            different. You don't talk about them.

MUMMY: Dem all watless.

DENISE: Ma!

MUMMY: (*Sucks teeth.*) Jus' nah put down yuh drink,
            yuh hear.

            *MUMMY digs out a Bible from her
            suitcase and hands it to DENISE.*

MUMMY: Here, mi want you fi read from it.

DENISE: Ma, no. They probably already have
            someone—and I don't even…

MUMMY: Denise!

DENISE: Whatever.

            *While looking through the Bible, pictures
            are stuck in the pages. DENISE examines
            them.*

DENISE: It's like we're strangers…'cept we all look alike. Same arms…legs—

Thick, muscle-y meat, tick, strong. Broad, heavy feet. Thighs full spilling over sides of chairs when flattened—

MUMMY: Denise, man! Hurry an' ready.

DENISE: I told you, I'm not going.

MUMMY: Jus' come nah!

DENISE: No.

MUMMY: Dee/eenise.

DENISE: /No!

MUMMY: Yah 'fraid?

DENISE: It's gross, I don't need to see Mayvie just laid out like that. Besides, don't they hire people to do that?

MUMMY: Dem nah do it right. Plus dem charge too much.

                    A moment.

DENISE: Miss her?

MUMMY: *(Sucks teeth.)* She nevah raise me. Me did raise with my granny. Mayvie wasn't a loving person, yuh know? Dis here gwan be most time I spend with ar' in…Since me come a foreign. Dis here will be the most time. She nevah act like a maddah, but maybe when me look 'pon ar'…Me nah even tink we favah each other. Nevah feel any'ting really fi ar' so…

                    Beat.

You have any lipstick?

DENISE: Since when you …ya, here.

> *DENISE puts the lipstick on her mother. This is a first.*

Stop shaking.

Relax the lips

Go "mah"

Rub

Kay.

You look nice.

MUMMY: It look good?

DENISE: Yeah. Wait.

> *DENISE gets her phone.*

MUMMY: You stay and help fix up in di kitchen.

DENISE: I can't cook. I'll just get in everyone's way. Besides, my head is killing—

MUMMY: So, you gwan stay lock up inna di room? Have them talk bad bout you? Get up man, *(Sucks teeth.)* cha!

> *DENISE holds up her camera phone without warning and takes a picture of her mother.*

How it turn out? It ugly?

DENISE: 'Course not.

MUMMY: *(Looking at the photo.)* Lawd, dat how me face stay suh? Boi my ugly!

DENISE:	Well, your eyes are closed, but it's cute. Besides, I have no pictures of you.
MUMMY:	Go give dis to Charm. *(MUMMY hands DENISE a blue scarf.)* She in di shop.
DENISE:	This is mine!
MUMMY:	You neva wear it, you cyan buy a next one / you have so many
DENISE:	/ Ya, but I still—forget it, fine.

DENISE examines the scarf, smells it. UNCLE PASON enters. He is long and dark and is always sweating. He has a gold cap in his front tooth and is still wearing his dirty work clothes.

UNCLE PASON:	*(Knocking while entering.)* Yuh decent?!!
MUMMY:	Come in.
DENISE:	Hi.
UNCLE PASON:	A who dis?!
DENISE:	Um…Denise.
UNCLE PASON:	Dis here Denise? …Lawd, look at you! Whoaaa di batty, yuh good boi, you nice an' tick, man! Yuh grow up nice. You look smart and nice. Ya have boyfriend?!
MUMMY:	You know she nah have no time fi dat. She a focus on her studies…
DENISE:	Ma, I finished school five years ago.
UNCLE PASON:	Ohhhhhweeee, so yuh have boyfriend?! *(Laughing.)* Mummy dat der is your baby, she nah let you go!
DENISE:	…I know.

UNCLE PASON:	Mayvie woulda see you grow up nice.
MUMMY:	(*Under her breath.*) She coulda come a foreign' plenty.
UNCLE PASON:	You know Mummy, though.
MUMMY:	(*Biting her tongue.*) Eh-he.
DENISE:	(*To UNCLE PASON.*) Can I? ...What...um happened?
MUMMY:	She just take sick.
DENISE:	How?
MUMMY:	The doctors here always killing off people. Dem always a cut people open.
UNCLE PASON:	Nah man, she did complain a long time 'bout her foot a pain ar' it swell up bad bad. Doctor say dem woulda have fi cut it. Next day she wake up an' cyan move, face numb, peeing up herself.
MUMMY:	Can'cah.
UNCLE PASON:	Nah, man—
MUMMY:	Dem mussa give ar' something—
UNCLE PASON:	She did have a stroke, man.
	A moment.
MUMMY:	She neva tell me she was sick. She neva say word, only a beg fi money—
DENISE:	Ma.
	MUMMY sucks her teeth.
UNCLE PASON:	Well, it nice you here, man. Death bring family togeda, e?

A beat.

UNCLE PASON: Come, yuh ready?

MUMMY: Me come'n. Denise a stay and help out.

UNCLE PASON: You 'fraid a duppy?

DENISE: No...I—

UNCLE PASON: Nah worry, Mummy will be happy you here. Yuh cyan' sing a liccle sinting at—

DENISE: Whoa, I don't sing.

UNCLE PASON: When yuh liccle, you did sing all di time. Yuh was cute—

DENISE: That wasn't real.

UNCLE PASON: Yuh too big now, e?

A strange silence passes.

Charm! It aright, go help Charm cook fi tonight. You can cook?

DENISE: Y—

UNCLE PASON: Charm, man! Come nah! *(To MUMMY.)* Aright, me a drive you, come.

MUMMY and UNCLE PASON start to head off.

UNCLE PASON: *(To MUMMY.)* A whaddat? Lipstick? *(Laughs.)*

MUMMY gives UNCLE PASON cut-eye and sucks her teeth. DENISE is left alone in the room. She sits on the bed. There is knocking on the bedroom door. DENISE hurries to stuff the scarf back into her luggage.

DENISE: Coming!

> *DENISE rises to her feet and leaves the room only to enter back on the other side (as if walking in a circle). VENUS' soundscape grows louder the further DENISE walks away from reality.*

Seven Night: Denise + Venus

> *VENUS stands atop her cage.*

VENUS: Heavy-heart-mess

Elbows deep

No more faking sleep

Rise to your feet.

DENISE: Charm?

VENUS: Come close.

DENISE: You…No…not again.

VENUS: Look at me.

Gaze into

With

Fall if you need to

DENISE: Your smell, your body, your voice… the way words bubble-wash *over your lips.*

VENUS: We

DENISE: …are you?

> *VENUS lowers herself to the floor.*

VENUS: Danced together, yes, we are not strangers.

I've been nestled in the grooves and dips where your hips define space

Within the folds of your flesh that you curse out of existence.

We are not strangers

I am your flesh, your blood,

though not how you take that to mean in this world.

There is no separation between mine and your time on this earth

We are not strangers

I take many shapes and makes and live in the world where ancestors watch, waiting for you to wake

We are not strangers

Because I am your ma, mami water, mother. The water that makes up most of your body.

You can try shut me out but water always has a way of leaking its way in.

 Beat.

VENUS:	It's okay.
DENISE:	No, it's not... I hate crying. This, now?
VENUS:	Because you need me the most now.
DENISE:	I don't need anything. This is not a good time.
VENUS:	This is the best time.

DENISE:	I can't ...I am just here to bury my grandmother and go back home. This cannot happen. I cannot fall apart away from home.
VENUS:	Why?
DENISE:	There is no one here for me.
VENUS:	This is the closest to home you've ever been.
DENISE:	This is not my home. They call me "foreignah"...thinking I'm rich. It doesn't feel like home.
VENUS:	You are closer than you think.

DENISE examines VENUS still in disbelief, but also completely mesmerized. She drops to the ground.

DENISE:	Looking at you makes my chest heavy.
VENUS:	That's a good thing. It's starting.
DENISE:	My death?
VENUS:	Your beginning. You are slowly opening. Coming into focus, parts filling back in.
DENISE:	Something's cracked inside me—
VENUS:	Yes, cracked open.
DENISE:	This has all been too much for my headheartmouth to understand.

A moment.

VENUS:	Time heals, but it also makes forgetting easy.
DENISE:	You forget so you can survive.

VENUS: How does it feel to survive when you are constantly pushing away pain? You have done a good job keeping distractions around.

Lurking, gazing, replacing, memorizing others' bodies—

DENISE: Searching for something familiar—

VENUS: But you don't know what you are looking for.

DENISE: I do and I don't. I know when I see it. Like with you. I see you and I see parts of myself. I remind myself I exist.

The cage swings open. VENUS leads DENISE inside.

Eight Night: Birth Of "The Hottentot Venus"

1810. London, England. DENISE watches from inside the cage, eyes peeping out the holes. She mirrors everything VENUS does. VENUS role-plays her past—and as she does, she transforms into the woman SARA BAARTMAN.

VENUS: Watching myself waiting.

Chest—rise fall rise pump tick click…

Cage

Holes big enough to stick my arm through

Head

She tries.

Leg

She tries.

No.
They build me a cage too small.

> *VENUS becomes SARA. SARA rocks the cage side to side.*

SARA:

Rocks to water crash pump thrash,

Like a desperate explorer daring the water goddess.

Don't swallow me up and spit me to shore,

Keep me afloat, bouncing off curvy waves,

'Cause home is too far away.

(To DENISE.) Our skin can hold everything in place, this skin is thick,

hard, calloused, blackened, and cracked.

Blocks the sun and can surely block a gaze.

Faces stare back at me. Eyes big and unblinking, mouth wide and dry.

Too many faces to see each one properly and hands chubby and pink palms out, out and up. I have to touch them to move past them, no path will be cleared. I have to touch—

Press, slither through them to get to the other side.

Hop-skip-jump

Safe now. I'm safe now safe now.

> *A beat.*

Drink the old me away and let the new bubble rise rise up Old "little Sara" left when I placed my hot foot in this cold cage.

DENISE: Where are we?

SARA: These cold stoney walls of London make me pine for home. The dirt here has no colour. Same with the food...and the people/the people

DENISE: /The People here talk without looking at one another.

SARA: Shallow voices slide through twisted teeth.

I try to decode their speech.

They speak two languages at the same time, what is said, and what they mean to say.

Back home, *they* would be put on display.

Their/

DENISE: /pink skin

SARA: betrays their emotions. *Pink skin,* that is not smart enough to hide blue and purple veins from their enemies' gaze. They would grow weary, nervous and faint.

Here women battle their dresses, shoes, hats, hair, skin, their body. They point and cackle at me, then turn around to stuff their skirt backs to have puffed-out posteriors.

whitewine make mountain wide thighs quiver shake seize grip tight.

Can't sneak a peek

I'll seal shut you tight.

Next time you put me in a cage, I'll bite.

To breathe a new world into an old story.

    Beat.

Tight, tight, tight.

We are master trick-sisters of changing our bodies to make them nicer to our eyes.

    Beat.

This reminds me of home even though we lived very separate lives all we have to remind each other of home is—

    CESAR enters.

We even smell different, look, dress

CESAR: Feel, taste…

    CESAR touches SARA's thigh.

SARA: to remind each other of—

CESAR: Where we came from.

SARA: It is dangerous to forget—

CESAR: What you are.

SARA: Make me.

CESAR: With my hands?

SARA: Mouth.

CESAR: Promise.

SARA   Come.

CESAR slowly kisses SARA's lips, then slides his lips across her face to her ear and down her neck. DENISE is trying hard not to swallow so loud.

SARA: Slow, slow, slow. Let your licks linger.

CESAR: Your hips smell of Africa!

SARA: All of Africa?

CESAR: The stretches of every shoreline.

SARA: Taste me.

He does. CESAR comes up for air, but his hands are still at work.

CESAR: Home.

Do you miss home? If I put my ear on your stomach, will I hear the stomping of the elands? How about your legs, if I press my hand over, up, up, up.

I am your MC. There is no show without me.

He abruptly pulls away and wipes hands.

If I stay, I will grow to despise you and myself, even more than I do.

Beat.

My, my, my... how the Venus has risen above us all. So far she floats high into the skies, floating past city lights. The fall will be a dangerous one.

SARA: Too bad you won't be there to catch me.

CESAR: I would never. I have done enough for you. Back home and now here. I will not sacrifice any more of myself. No wife, no child, my life back home is impossible to have again here. You are a curse. Nothing good will come from you. Oh, and when this all stops, I will keep far from your wiggles and quakes.

SARA: You are jealous, Cesar. It does not suit you, friend.

CESAR: I am not your friend.

SARA: Brother?

CESAR: ...

SARA: Then what?

> *CESAR removes his MC jacket and transforms into the British DR. ALEXANDER DUNLOP who was credited as discovering "The Hottentot Venus." He is giving a lecture. Each time DR. DUNLOP touches DENISE, She has no control over what she says.*

Eight Night/ Part B: Lecture

> *London, England, 1811. DR. ALEXANDER DUNLOP among his colleagues, inside a packed operating theatre. DENISE plays DOCTOR 1. SARA BAARTMAN is centre, facing his audience.*

DR. DUNLOP: This medical condition, known as ...

DOCTOR 1: St-steat-e-yo-

DR. DUNLOP: Steatopygia. Gluteal and femoral obesity; predominant in all Hottentot women.

DOCTOR 1:   Extensive research must be done before we can draw—

DR. DUNLOP: The research I have compiled is of lived experience, not from a medical journal. Gentlemen, I assure you, what I have seen in my travels is unaccounted for. To note the obvious physical ailments that afflict Hottentot women is only a superficial observation that lacks critical comparative analysis and contextualization. While in my time living in South Africa, I witnessed and encountered a diverse range of peoples. I learned that the Hottentots are of the Khoisan tribe. They are some of the earliest inhabitants of that land. Hottentot women are closest to nature, the primate. The fatty tissue that surrounds the thighs and posteriors of the Hottentot women has no clear function. Perhaps the most striking feature of these women is the "apron" that can be seen—

DOCTOR 1:   Apron?

DR. DUNLOP: The elongated labia that—

    Beat.

    Her vagina must hang like the neck of a chicken; I wonder if it clucks? If it thumps, slaps, and clicks against her thighs as she walks? A seductress who refuses to show *that* part of herself, the absurdity. The thickness of her thighs is unlike anything I have ever seen. But the girth and weight does not compare to the size of her...posterior. I cannot keep my eyes off this part of her body. There are so many unanswered questions when I look at her. From her short wool-textured hair, pressed nose, inflamed lips that part to reveal luminous pearls. My eyes scan every inch of her repeatedly. Forever sketched in my head Look, it is quite fascinating, isn't it?

Her shape is unlike anything I have ever laid eyes on.

DOCTOR 1:   She must be of a separate race from the Negroes. Only a detailed comparison could give us the findings we need to prove her kind to sit at the lowest race of humans—the Negro race. Or among the highest race of monkeys, the orangutan.

> *DENISE tries to take off her doctor's coat. It is stuck on her.*

DENISE: *(Tears thick in her throat.)* Please. Stop...

DR. DUNLOP: She emerges from the thick greens of her land. Red dirt still resting in her little toes.

Her body is the danger and mystery of her continent.

A Venus.

My Venus.

> *DR. DUNLOP kisses VENUS on the face and exits.*

SARA: *Height 4 feet 9 inches.*

Hips 18 inches or 45.72 cm.

Protrusion of the posterior 19.3 cm or 7.6 in.

That is the only one that counts.

Drawing lines on my skin, holding tape, wrapping ribbon round my thighs, calf, hips, my hips, waist, inseam, bust, shoulders, arm span, the inseam, my hips, neck, head, head to waist, waist to crotch, crown to crotch, they want to see how long it danglejangles if it's true, if its shaped like they see in their hungry dreams.

Standing on foot for hours. They wrap tape round my head and scribble on my skin, 'cept my skin is not their white blank sheets of paper. My stomach grumbles and no longer quiets on its own. A sharp pain in my side gets worse with each day. I ask for medicine in a room full of doctors and they all stare.

My skin takes their print. They want me to wince, squint, twitch, showing I am in pain—I am still so still so still like stone. I know what they want me to do and I feel my mouth water—my body wants to spit. My body is preparing itself to spit a long, wet string of spit to hit them with.

I swallow it. So many of my words, I swallow. Sometimes I forget that my stomach is empty because my belly is big with words.

DENISE rips off the doctor's coat.

DENISE:

I'm sorry, I didn't know what was coming out my mouth. I wanted to stop, I wanted to smash all those ugly words he was saying and kick-scream-punch myself. I can't believe those words came from these lips. They were not my words, you know they were not my words.

VENUS: You did nothing wrong. I have already heard all those words, they have done their damage.

DENISE: I don't have thick Black woman skin like you. I don't know how to let their words not cut my skin.

VENUS: No skin is thick enough to keep those cuts away.

> *DR. GEORGE CUVIER enters. (The French doctor who was responsible for dissecting Sara Baartman's body. He is played by CESAR.) As he speaks, more silver instruments fall from the sky into his hands.*
>
> *A pregnant SARA is washing clothes in the river, back home Eastern Cape, South Africa. (Choreography in CAPITAL LETTERS may be read and enacted, or simply enacted.)*

CUVIER: This little blade can open up a world of mysteries, confirm discoveries, and prove hypotheses.

SARA: *IN, DOWN, TOGETHER, OUT*

CUVIER: This thin blade can reach into the past, finding a diamond behind the muck.

SARA: *LIFT HIGH, THEN SLAP, SQUEEZE*

                LET THE WATER OUT, AND DRIP OUT THE

                WEIGHT

CUVIER: It is a key—

DENISE: No.

CUVIER:	My key into the human body. Nowhere is forbidden to me.
SARA:	*WRING*
DENISE:	Stop.
SARA:	*SLAP*
CUVIER:	Bodies lie before me—
SARA:	*SQUEEZE*
CUVIER:	Begging me to discover them.
DENISE:	Please!
SARA:	*(To the baby in her belly.)* You love the water—
CUVIER:	I give them stories and make them famous on my shelves.
SARA:	Show Mumma how you like to kick and stretch your little—

Belly too cold. You need to move to warm yourself up.

There is no movement.

Do not be lazy.

Head...bum...back...

Too still. Still cold.

Frozen.

CLICK- CRACKLE-CRACK

SARA's belly begins to splinter.

Let Mumma see

NO NO NOOOOOOO will get every little piece of you and return you to where you come from. GO GO GOOOOOOO back in

The cloth that SARA was washing earlier has now become SARA's unresponsive baby girl.

I lied, baby, and I am sorry.

When I spoke words of protecting you, I did not think it would be so hard. Let Mumma clean you up. I want to eat my words. What colour are your eyes? Let Mumma see.

SARA opens her baby's eye.

Brown, but not too dark, like a beige. Beige eyes. Open your little mouth. Let Mumma see.

SARA opens the baby's mouth with her thumb.

Your little pink tongue. Poke out and point and flatten—come now. Do it.

A moment.

Her baby remains unresponsive.

Pull and tug on my fingers.

SARA lifts the baby's hand and places the little fingers around her pointer finger.

SARA: You have a weak grip. You did not get that from me.

weh...weh

we will have to have to to to

wo-wo work on that and build up some strength.

SARA kisses her baby's forehead.

Look at all this hair!

DENISE slowly moves to SARA and her baby. SARA starts digging into the ground.

DENISE: I'm so…

DENISE gets down and starts digging beside SARA. Music whips around both women. Remnants of the many sounds we've heard up till now; waves crashing, low rumble of a bass, layered with traces of SARA's water song, the clanging of CUVIER's metal and stomping of VENUS' dancing builds to crescendo. SARA places her baby in the ground. Both women water the soil with their tears. SARA transforms back into VENUS.

DENISE: How does your face even remember to smile?

VENUS: Help me look for stones. Cannot have unmarked graves.

DENISE helps VENUS gather stones.

DENISE: How many have you lost?

VENUS: They are not "lost." They are all right here. I bury them myself. They will become part of the earth now. They keep growing that way.

I have many daughters.

Their bones birth thick trunks and bright leaves

Black branches that house bright ripe fruit

Use them for nourishment and grow crown high

Thick, muscley meat, stretched, round round

Flat-footed pounds crack ground to make space for light to—

DENISE: There is no light! All the terrible things you had to live through. Separated, kept in jars, forgotten in pieces…

VENUS: It must be hard to see through all that fire.

DENISE: How are your eyes not hot?

VENUS: I couldn't be here if they were.

If my eyes were still hot with blood, I could not have brought you here

I could not help you wake up.

A cage. A mirror. Both held up behind glass.

I am lucky now.

I have seen all the beauty your world didn't allow me and so much more

I am a mother to many daughters, and in turn,

I am a daughter to mami wata.

She taught me to…

Press play.

Hop-skip-jump.

Growl, roar, run, stomp, rumble shake the
earth with all my might and run in place so
hard so fast like hordes of eland coming to
swallow all the hurt.

Play!

Make a game of it

Hop from rock to land, back up to rock.

Maintain my balance and promise not to
drop.

Freeze while wide eyed bright and awake

See all my children that passed through me

The ones I sneak a peek and the ones that
rest under my feet

I get close enough to

Lift them

float up on toesies

Fliiiiiiiiiight!

    A beat.

I have peace because I need to. That depth
of darkness is unbearable for any living
thing to carry over.

DENISE: So you aren't sad?

VENUS: Not in the same way you are.

All my children that rest under our feet
made me mothers to so many others. If
I don't have daughters, the story is for
nothing.

Venus touches the TORTOISE necklace on DENISE. There is a warm heartbeat.

DENISE now understands what VENUS has been trying to teach her all along. VENUS exits.

DENISE follows and stops.

DENISE: *I didn't love you for so long.*

I'm not sure I can feel all the love I'm trying to force into myself. I'm hoping over time it will seep in.

This new love may have nothing to latch itself to and make buddies with—so I'll have to water it a lot, and give it plenty of good food.

I want this love to grow so it can bust me open

like...

Hungry warrior—radically taking up all space—

kind of love.

Thickly imprinting every slap, blap, dab from thunder thighs—kind of love.

Ride or die commitment to constantly choosing to stay awake—

kind of love

To love my own, instead of looking to other.

Seeking truth through these beautiful almond eyes

I know for a fact came from my great-great-grandmother.

> *DENISE removes the tortoise necklace, presses it to her lips and places it on the ground.*

i press play

i hop

i skip.

> *DENISE jumps into...*

> *Blackout.*

> *End of play.*

Timeline of Significant Events

- 1652–1795: Dutch East India Company (VOC) has control over Cape Town, South Africa.

- 1770s: Baartman's year of birth is within this decade. Gamtoos River Valley, South Africa.

- 1795–96: Sara is sold to Pieter Cesar, Hendrik Cesar's brother.

- 1799–1802: "Hottentot" Rebellion. Fought between the British and the African Indigenous (Khoikhoi and amaXhosa) populations in Southern Africa.

- 1807: Ban on the transatlantic slave trade within the British empire.

- 1809: Sara travels from South Africa to Europe along with Hendrik Cesar and Dr. Alexander Dunlop (Scottish ship's surgeon) and two slave boys.

- 1809: Caledon Code was implemented by Cape Governor Lord Caledon. A law which prevented colonists from removing Khoekhoe from the Cape.

- 1810: Baartman is first exhibited in London, England at 225 Piccadilly Circus, Egyptian Hall.

- 1810: In November, Zachary Macaulay (English abolitionist) pursues legal action against Dunlop and Cesar. The King's Bench questions Baartman's free will regarding being exhibited in England. After Baartman testifies she is there of her own accord, the case is closed.

- 1814: Baartman is sold to an animal trainer Reaux in Paris, France.

- 1815: On December 31, Baartman dies in Paris, likely of pneumonia.

- 1815: Within hours of Baartman's death, her brain, genitals and skeleton are removed and preserved during a dissection performed by French scientist George Cuvier.

- 1834: Slavery is abolished in the Cape.

- 1937: Baartman's remains are exhibited in the Musée de l'Homme.

- 1994: Baartman's remains are moved from Musée de l'Homme to Musee d'Orsay.

- 1994: South African president Nelson Mandela formally requests that Baartman's remains be removed from Musée de l'Homme and returned to South Africa.

- 2002: In August, Sara Baartman's remains are returned to South Africa and buried.

- 2010: In October, South Africa's Department of Arts and Culture announces a plan for the Sara Baartman Center of Remembrance, a museum in Hankey Eastern Cape, South Africa.

"Sara Baartman's 1810 exhibition in London embodies, literally, the transition between the older tradition of freak shows and the merging nineteenth-century desire for evidence of the ethnographic 'real' and the rise of a bourgeois consumer culture of the exotic." (From *Sara Baartman and the Hottentot Venus: A Ghost Story and a Biography* by Clifton Crais and Pamela Scully)

"...It is often interpreted that Baartman's nickname, "Hottentot Venus," reflects a contradiction in beauty and freakery. In her study of socially constructed disabled bodies in freak shows, Rosemarie Garland Thomson suggests that this title served to create a "frightening paradox": "one term perverts the other: the 'Hottentot,' which signified to the Western mind savagery and irredeemable physiological inferiority, is paired with 'Venus,' the West's apotheosis of femininity." (From *Venus in Dark* by Janell Hobson)

Glossary

DUPPY: Refers to the disembodied spirits which linger around the community after someone passes. The word duppy (*dupon*) comes from the Ghanaian language Twi and refers to the roots of a large tree.

FREED BLACK: Hendrik Cesar and his family were the last family who owned Sara Baartman in South Africa. They were part of a small community of Free Blacks who were born into slavery and were later manumitted.

HOTTENTOT: (Dutch) A derogatory word used to describe Khoikhoi (and Khoisans) by Dutch settlers in the 17th century. The word derived from the German term "hotteren-totteren" which translates to "stutter." This was used to reference the click sounds within the Khoikhoi (and Khoisan) language.

KHOEKHOE: Khoekhoe and San (Khoisan) people were the first pre-colonial inhabitants of Southwestern Africa.

NINE NIGHT: A Jamaican wake where family and friends of the deceased gather for nine nights to celebrate their life. The sharing of food and drinks are to ensure the duppy (spirit) gets a proper send-off. This custom is practised throughout much of the Caribbean and has its roots in Yoruba tradition.

Further Reading

- *Venus in the Dark: Blackness and Beauty in Popular Culture* by Janell Hobson (Routledge, 2005).
- *Sara Baartman and the Hottentot Venus: A Ghost Story and a Biography* by Clifton Crais and Pamela Scully (Princeton University Press, 2009).
- *Fearing the Black Body: The Racial Origins of Fat Phobia* by Sabrina Strings (NYU Press, 2019).
- *Venus in Two Acts* by Saidiya Hartman (In *Small Axe: a Caribbean journal of Criticism*, Duke University Press, 2009).